BE A SCIENTIST!

Be A
COMPUTER SCIENTIST

BY JONATHAN E. BARD

 Gareth Stevens
PUBLISHING

Please visit our website, www.garethstevens.com. For a free color catalog of all our high-quality books, call toll free 1-800-542-2595 or fax 1-877-542-2596.

Library of Congress Cataloging-in-Publication Data

Names: Bard, Jonathan, author.
Title: Be a computer scientist / Jonathan Bard.
Description: New York : Gareth Stevens Publishing, [2019] | Series: Be a
   scientist! | Includes index.
Identifiers: LCCN 2018014475| ISBN 9781538229958 (library bound) | ISBN
   9781538231173 (pbk.) | ISBN 9781538231234 (6 pack)
Subjects: LCSH: Computer science–Vocational guidance–Juvenile literature.
Classification: LCC QA76.25 .B36 2019 | DDC 004.023–dc23
LC record available at https://lccn.loc.gov/2018014475

First Edition

Published in 2019 by
Gareth Stevens Publishing
111 East 14th Street, Suite 349
New York, NY 10003

Copyright © 2019 Gareth Stevens Publishing

Designer: Katelyn E. Reynolds
Editor: Monika Davies

Photo credits: Cover, p. 1 sanjeri/E+/Getty Images; cover, pp. 1–32 (background image) lucadp/
Shutterstock.com; p. 5 Anna Hoychuk/Shutterstock.com; p. 7 chaipanya/Shutterstock.com; p. 9 Westend61/
Getty Images; p. 13 REDPIXEL.PL/Shutterstock.com; p. 15 baranozdemir/E+/Getty Images; p. 17 courtesy
of NASA; pp. 19, 27 wavebreakmedia/Shutterstock.com; p. 21 Iurii Stepanov/Shutterstock.com; p. 23 Thomas
Barwick/Stone/Getty Images; p. 25 Katherine Frey/The Washington Post via Getty Images; p. 29 Kiyoshi Ota/
Bloomberg via Getty Images.

Printed in the United States of America

CPSIA compliance information: Batch #CW19GS: For further information contact Gareth Stevens, New York, New York at 1-800-542-2595.

CONTENTS

WORDS IN THE GLOSSARY APPEAR IN **BOLD** TYPE
THE FIRST TIME THEY ARE USED IN THE TEXT.

COMPUTERS

Computers are everywhere. They are in our phones, our cars, and now even our refrigerators! They can keep track of how many steps we take, how fast our hearts beat, and even how much we eat. But did you know that computers can't do any of these things without people called computer scientists?

Computer scientists are people who design and build computers to help us accomplish a variety of our goals. These scientists study how to make computers faster and stronger, and they write programs we all use and enjoy every day.

THE FIRST "COMPUTER"

The word "computer" was first used in 1613, way before the modern computer was built! The word was originally used to describe a person who did math calculations, and it kept this definition until electronic computers started to do the math instead of people.

<Outdoor Cycle 7:28

− 400 +

SET CALORIES

Start

LEARNING TO CODE

The first step to becoming a computer scientist is learning how to write code. Code is the set of instructions computers need to do everything. Every task a computer completes uses a different code. For example, one code tells your computer to run your favorite program, and a different code lets you send messages to your friends.

COMPUTER CHATTER

Many **coding languages** are used around the world, and it's almost impossible to count them all. Some languages are used only by the people who created them! Each coding language has its own style and syntax, or rules. This is like rules in written languages, such as how sentences in English start with a capital letter and end with a period.

Learning how to code can be easy! Many programmers start with a program called "Hello, World!" This program tells the computer to say hello in a message box. Programmers begin with this program because it gives a visible result. They know they've correctly programmed when they see the message box.

C programming

```
#include <stdio.h>

int main() {
 printf("Hello, World!");
 return 0;
}
```

Hello, World!

Java programming

```
public class Main {
    public static void main(String[] args) {
        System.out.println("Hello, World!");
    }
}
```

Hello, World!

7

CHOOSING A PATH

While taking classes and learning all about computers, programming students start to figure out what interests them. During their college education, students are encouraged to **specialize**. If they like biology or medicine, they may choose to focus on the field of bioinformatics. If they are interested in keeping data safe, they can take classes to become security analysts.

Students are also encouraged to complete internships. This is when a student works for a company to gain real-life work experience before they graduate. It's helpful for students to take different classes and complete internships as they learn about the different careers available to them.

WHAT INTERESTS YOU?

Computer scientists have different interests. Some enjoy working on math equations, and others are more interested in **biology**. Some love video games, and others want to design and program websites. The best part about computer science is that the options are nearly endless, since computers are used for so many things!

INTERNSHIPS ALLOW STUDENTS TO TEST OUT WHAT A JOB WILL BE LIKE. STUDENTS ARE THEN ABLE TO SEE IF A CERTAIN CAREER OR FIELD IS RIGHT FOR THEM.

9

KEEPING THINGS RUNNING:
SYSTEM ADMINISTRATORS

Computers need to be set up, managed, and maintained. Computer scientists who specialize in this are called system administrators. They make sure computers stay up and running, and that lets other people get their work done.

WHAT IS AN OPERATING SYSTEM?

Every computer has a main program that starts up when the computer is powered on. This is called an operating system, and it controls everything the computer does. Many different operating systems are available today. The two most popular are Windows and MacOS X.

System administrators need to know a lot about the operating systems they manage. For example, computers that use a Windows system don't run the same as computers that use an Apple system. Since systems are so different, a system administrator might choose to become an **expert** in one system over the others.

One of the most important jobs of all system administrators is making sure all of a computer's programs are up-to-date.

OPERATING SYSTEMS CURRENTLY IN USE*

DESKTOPS AND MOBILE DEVICES ALL AROUND THE WORLD USE DIFFERENT OPERATING SYSTEMS. DO YOU KNOW WHICH ONES YOUR FAMILY OR SCHOOL USES? SOME ARE MORE POPULAR THAN OTHERS!

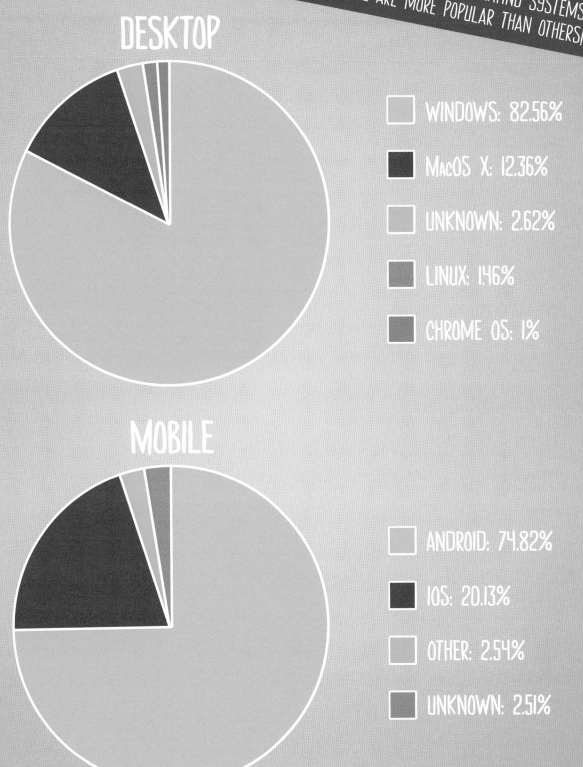

DESKTOP

- WINDOWS: 82.56%
- MacOS X: 12.36%
- UNKNOWN: 2.62%
- LINUX: 1.46%
- CHROME OS: 1%

MOBILE

- ANDROID: 74.82%
- IOS: 20.13%
- OTHER: 2.54%
- UNKNOWN: 2.51%

*ACCORDING TO STATCOUNTER GLOBAL STATS, AS OF FEBRUARY 2018

WRITING CODE:
COMPUTER PROGRAMMERS

For computers to work how we want them to, they need to be programmed. The people who do this are called computer programmers, and they learn many coding languages to tackle all kinds of projects.

A lot of the work that goes into creating a program doesn't happen on a computer! First, a team of programmers discusses what the program needs to do, how the code should be written, and how the program will be made.

Once they have a plan, programmers write the code. They often work in teams of two, which helps them find errors and prevent **bugs** from getting into the final program.

TWO ARE BETTER THAN ONE

One popular way to prevent bugs in code is to program with a partner. Many programmers learned to program by themselves, so teaming up can take some getting used to. But pair programming has been proven to cut down on the number of errors, and it makes the final version of code better.

ALL PROGRAMMERS BENEFIT FROM HAVING SOMEONE ELSE LOOK AT THEIR CODE AND CHECK FOR ERRORS.

STORING INFORMATION: DATABASE ADMINISTRATORS

Computers can store a lot of information. To organize this information, computer scientists need databases. Every piece of data is kept in a particular spot in the database. This way when people need a piece of data, they can find it quickly. In this way, databases are a lot like libraries!

Computer scientists who specialize in creating and using databases are called database administrators. They often work for large businesses that have a lot of data to store. To start each project, database administrators think about what kind of data is being collected. Database administrators then write programs to organize the information so others can easily access the data.

DATA, DATA, DATA

Every business deals with a lot of data. This data can include details about products, customers, sales, and more! It's very important that this data is organized effectively. For example, a business might want to organize the contact information of its customers. A database administrator collects first names, last names, phone numbers, and mailing addresses, then sorts this information in a way that makes it easy to find.

SINCE THEY SOMETIMES WORK WITH PRIVATE OR PERSONAL INFORMATION, DATABASE ADMINISTRATORS ALSO MUST CONSIDER HOW TO PROTECT THE INFORMATION HOUSED IN THE DATABASES THEY CREATE.

15

PUSHING THE LIMITS: HARDWARE ENGINEERS

Computer scientists who look for new ways to make computers work better are called **hardware** engineers. They design, build, and test all the parts used when building computers.

Hardware engineers make sure all parts of a computer are compatible, meaning that the parts work well together. If the parts aren't compatible, it could be because some parts are older than others, or they might be made for one type of computer and not usable in others.

Another job of a hardware engineer is figuring out what kind of computer someone needs. Someone looking to check their email needs only a personal computer. A large agency such as NASA (National Aeronautics and Space Administration) might need a **supercomputer**!

MOORE'S LAW

In 1965, engineer Gordon Moore **predicted** that computer processing power, or the number of calculations a computer can do, would double every 2 years. Moore's law proved to be true for almost 50 years as hardware engineers pushed the limits of what was possible! Though improvements are still being made, progress is slowing down.

HELPING COMPUTERS TALK: NETWORK ENGINEERS

Computers need to be on the same network in order to communicate with each other. A network is a connection of at least two computers that exchange information. For example, a school likely has at least one network for all of its computers. Network engineers make sure a network is fast and stable so that the people using it can get their work done without issues.

If lots of devices are connected to the network at the same time, the network needs to be able to handle all that traffic. Network engineers set up networks to handle the demands of their users. They also need to be good at **troubleshooting** so they can solve problems that pop up!

IN DEMAND

More and more devices are being added to networks every day. These days, smartphones, smart fridges, and smart cars all connect to networks. Network engineers are constantly working to improve networks to support these new devices. Demand for computer scientists with networking skills is increasing as more smart devices are made.

KEEPING DATA SAFE: SECURITY ANALYSTS

Keeping data safe is important! So much of our personal information, including health care and banking records, is now online. Computer scientists who protect our information are called security analysts.

People who use their computer skills to steal information are known as hackers. Hackers write programs called **viruses**, and users may accidently download and run these programs. When they do, these viruses can take users' information and send it back to the hackers. Security analysts write **antivirus** programs that search users' computers to find viruses planted by hackers.

Many organizations employ security analysts to keep their information safe. Banks especially need to keep their data safe to protect people's money!

PROTECTIVE PASSWORDS

We can protect our information by using strong passwords for online accounts such as email and social media. A strong password has at least 12 characters and, more importantly, is never used for more than one account. That way, if one account gets hacked, other accounts stay protected.

WEAK, AVERAGE, AND STRONG PASSWORDS

STRONG PASSWORDS DO NOT USE AN INDIVIDUAL'S PERSONAL INFORMATION, LIKE NAMES, BIRTHDAYS, OR FAVORITE PLACES TO VACATION.

ISSUE	WEAK	AVERAGE	STRONG
TOO SHORT	Dog Cat Buffalo	DogCatBuffalo	DOgC@t$Buffalo
TOO COMMON	Password password1	betterIP@ssword	b3$tPa$$wOrds
USES PERSONAL INFORMATION	JaneDoe	CartwheelButterfly	Car7wheelButt3rfly

Username

user

Password

CREATING CONTENT:
WEB DEVELOPERS

Many of us love to browse the internet, from viewing funny cat videos to checking out educational websites when doing homework. But who builds our favorite websites? Computer scientists called web developers create every part of the websites we visit every day.

DEVELOPMENT LINGO

Three coding languages are found on many websites: HTML5, CSS, and JavaScript. Each coding language has a specific job to do. Think of a "like" button on social media. HTML5 determines where the button appears on a web page, while CSS decides what the button looks like. JavaScript controls what happens when you tap or click that button.

Web developers build websites for big companies, small organizations, and everything in between. They first have to think about how people will **interact** with the website. Then, they write code that both makes the website enjoyable for users to visit and encourages users to share it with family and friends. Before a website goes live, web developers also check every part of the site one more time in a process called quality assurance.

DURING THE QUALITY ASSURANCE PROCESS, WEB DEVELOPERS DOUBLE-CHECK THEIR WORK AND FIX ANY BUGS THEY MIGHT FIND.

23

STUDYING BIOLOGY:
BIOINFORMATICIANS

Computer scientists use their skills to try to solve all kinds of problems. Sometimes, these problems are deadly diseases. Bioinformaticians use computer science to study biology, including diseases such as cancer.

Bioinformaticians write programs that look at huge amounts of data from thousands of samples. They use math and statistics, or information that can be related in numbers, to find patterns in the data. For disease **research**, bioinformaticians work closely with doctors and other scientists. They want to learn how diseases start, and they try to figure out ways to help people living with illnesses.

WANTED: DATA OVERLOAD!

Every human being is unique, which makes understanding human biology very difficult. One way bioinformaticians find patterns in biological data is by looking at hundreds or even thousands of people's data all at once! To do this, they need supercomputers. A personal computer wouldn't be able to handle all of that data. It would likely **crash**!

ANOTHER IMPORTANT PART OF A BIOINFORMATICIAN'S JOB IS TO MANAGE AND ORGANIZE THE DATA THEY COLLECT.

MAKING TIME FOR FUN: GAME DEVELOPERS

Video games offer a fun way for many people to kick back and relax, but it actually takes a lot of work to create them! To make a video game, a number of different computer scientists have to work together to get the job done. Programmers write the code for the game, system administrators keep the game **servers** running, and network engineers make sure players can connect in from all around the world.

Creating a video game is a great example of how much teamwork goes into computer science. Since there are many different things to do, a video game project takes many people with different skills all working as a team.

LEARNING THE GAME

There are many different paths to becoming a game developer. As the video game industry continues to grow, many colleges offer degrees in video game development. Within these programs, you study how to design video games, as well as how to program these designs. And, of course, learning to work with a team of other developers is also part of these programs!

VIRTUAL REALITY IS AN EXCITING NEW AREA OF VIDEO GAMES THAT GAME DEVELOPERS ARE WORKING HARD AT IMPROVING!

THE FUTURE OF COMPUTERS: ARTIFICIAL INTELLIGENCE

As computers become smarter and faster, computer scientists have to push the limits of what we think computers can do. More and more scientists are turning to artificial intelligence, which teaches computers to "think" based on what they've done before. For example, as you type a text message, the computer can finish each word for you. The computer is using artificial intelligence to predict what you want to say!

SELF-DRIVING CARS

One exciting area of research that uses artificial intelligence is self-driving cars. These are cars that drive themselves. Cameras, tools that detect changes in the car's surroundings, and communication with other self-driving cars help make this possible. One day in the future, a driverless car might show up at your door, ready to take you wherever you need to go!

The future of computer science is exciting and full of opportunities. All around the world, computer scientists are programming new tools, creating exciting video games, and discovering medical breakthroughs. A computer scientist's work is always changing and developing, and this makes their job rewarding—and fun!

CARS HAVE SO MANY COMPUTER PROGRAMS IN THEM.
SOON THEY WILL EVEN DRIVE THEMSELVES!

GLOSSARY

antivirus: programs that detect computer viruses

biology: the science that studies living things

bug: an error in code

coding language: the language computer programmers use to instruct a computer

crash: when a computer or program fails

expert: someone who knows a great deal about something

hardware: the physical parts of a computer

interact: to act upon one another

predict: to guess what will happen in the future based on facts or knowledge

research: studying to find something new

server: the central computer that supplies data for the other computers to use

specialize: to become very good at one particular thing

supercomputer: many computers connected together to form a very strong computer

troubleshoot: to find problems

virus: a computer program that harms a computer

FOR MORE INFORMATION

BOOKS

Briggs, Jason. *Python for Kids: A Playful Introduction to Programming.* San Francisco, CA: No Starch Press Inc., 2013.

Liukas, Linda. *Hello Ruby: Adventures in Coding.* New York, NY: Feiwel and Friends, 2015.

Woodcock, Jon. *DK Workbooks: Computer Coding.* New York, NY: DK Children, 2014.

WEBSITES

Code.org
www.code.org
Code.org is a great general resource for learning to code with classes for all age levels.

Khan Academy
www.khanacademy.org/hourofcode
Khan Academy's Hour of Code is an easy way to dive into programming basics.

Scratch
www.scratch.mit.edu
Learn the basics of coding through MIT Media Lab's interactive games and storytelling.

INDEX